JESUS

FRIEND
TO
TERRORISTS

R. Wurmbrand

RADU VALENTIN

Jesus—Friend to Terrorists

© 1995 by The Voice of the Martyrs Inc.

Published by Living Sacrifice Book Company, a division of The Voice of the Martyrs, P.O. Box 2273, Bartlesville, OK 74005-2273.

For the security of the author, we have used a pseudonym for the author's name.

Library of Congress Cataloging-in-Publication Data
Valentin, Radu.
   Jesus : friend to terrorists / Radu Valentin.
        p.   cm.
   ISBN 0-88264-308-8
   1. Terrorism—Religious aspects—Christianity—Controversial literature.   2. Nonviolence—Religious aspects—Christianity.   3. Witness bearing (Christianity).
4. World politics—20th century.   I. Title.
BT736.15.W87   1995
241'.697—dc20   CIP

Contents

A Friend to Terrorists?

THE PERSON writing this is a Christian pastor. For decades I have followed the actions, pronouncements and, where they existed, the publications of terrorist groups in different countries.

Today, I realize that mankind has entered a new age. The era of Fascist domination has passed. The age when the Soviet dictator representing the Eastern Communist bloc could tell Americans "We will bury you!" has also passed. The cold war has passed to the history books. We have now entered the age of terrorism.

Terrorist groups have mushroomed on all continents and claim dedicated supporters and sympathizers.

Most people react to them with horror as headlines assault them from all over the world. How should Christians react?

I tell my fellow Christians that we should consider terrorists our friends. To the terrorists themselves who read this, I say, "I am your friend and the friend of those who think like you."

Most Christians will disagree strongly, saying, "We've never heard anything like this. Should we be the friends of murderers? So many were killed or wounded in the attack on the World Trade Center in New York. So many are killed in Peru, Egypt, Algeria, Israel, India, South

5

Africa, the United Kingdom, Latin America, and
other countries. Why should we call the terrorists 'friends'?"

The devil plays the role of accuser. ("Devil"
comes from the Greek *diabolos*, which means "to
hurl accusations against.") It is written that Jesus
is "the friend of sinners" (Matthew 11:19), in-
cluding thieves, adulterers, traitors, and murderers.

The night before His crucifixion, Jesus
called His disciples "friends," then went out of
His way to confer this title also on Judas Iscariot,
who had departed the group to betray Him. He
called Judas "friend" when Judas already had the
price of betrayal—30 pieces of silver, his traitor's
reward—in his pocket and came with soldiers to
arrest Him (Matthew 26:48–50).

We don't know much about Judas, some
believe "Iscariot" is from the Hebrew *Ish Kerioth*,
which means "man of Kerioth." But there is
another possibility. In Jesus' time was a group of
Jewish terrorists called *Sikkarim*, which means
"men of the dagger." They used this weapon
against their Roman oppressors and also against
Jewish collaborators. Iscariot could have belonged to this group.

Had Judas been a terrorist who was received
kindly by Jesus, but later had a controversy with
Him that led him, in a moment of extreme
anger, to play the part of traitor? When Jesus was
convicted in a mock trial, Judas regretted his
rash act and, full of remorse, committed suicide.

So for a brief period at least, a terrorist emotionally identified with Jesus.

This explanation might seem far-fetched if it were not for the fact that Jesus had named as an apostle a man called Simon the Zealot. Zealots too were extreme Jewish nationalists who resorted to the use of force against the Roman oppressors. Also, the apostle Peter in Gethsemane was armed, and he was not the only armed apostle (Luke 22:38). Although Simon may have been a terrorist, he was not a terrorist during his discipleship, and was approached by Jesus as a friend. And so Christians, thinking about these parts of the Bible, might not be surprised that I address this book to "terrorist friends."

Are Terrorists Totally Wrong?

IBELIEVE IT is totally wrong to consider anyone totally wrong.

Jesus, referring to those who would persecute believers down through the ages, said, "Those who kill you will believe that they are serving God" (John 16:2). Many inquisitors of different confessions (Catholics were not the only ones to use inquisitorial methods against believers with whom they differed) adored the Savior and intended to please Him with their acts.

We should not wonder about this. Many personalities of the Old Testament acted in a strange manner that no Christian would imitate and with the firm conviction that they were doing God's will. Perhaps this was the case with those who built the Tower of Babel, whose objective was never possible (Genesis 11:1–9).

Jesus makes a difference between the "why" and the "what" of a person's actions. Some persecute Christians because they erroneously believe that Christians are wrong. The Christian New Testament, part of our holy book, tells about a Jew full of zeal for God who participated in the stoning of a Christian named Stephen. Both heartily loved God but had different levels of knowledge of Him. Later, Saul of Tarsus accepted the religion of his victim Stephen and also died as a martyr for Christ. They must have met again in the same beautiful heaven.

Today's terrorists are convinced that they serve well their nation, religion, race, or party. We may wholeheartedly agree with them that one should do his utmost in the service of these entities. Thus we have a point of contact.

In differences between men it is good to stress the points that unite them. When Christians confront the thinking of those with other convictions, they should not always ask themselves first, "What separates me from the other man?" but "In what ways are we in agreement?"

On a certain occasion, the apostle Paul, a dedicated Christian, spoke in Athens, Greece to a crowd of men who worshiped gods that he despised as idols. Yet he does not begin by telling them what was wrong about their beliefs. Instead he says, "I found you to be very religious" (Acts 17:22). Paul had something in common with those he wished to criticize. The Athenians knew *correctly* that there was something superior to be worshiped.

Knowing that every point of view is a point of blindness because it incapacitates one for every other point of view, we should keep an open mind even for those with whom we disagree. All of us, Christian and non-Christian alike, know only in part. Therefore, we can't speak to one another condescendingly as the wise to the ignorant. And so we ask you to recognize your own limitations, as we do ours, and listen to a voice different from what you are accustomed to hearing.

Are you a terrorist because you consider your cause the best? Do you say to yourself, "There is no better cause for which I can give my life and, if necessary, take another's life?"

I once spoke with a fanatical Zionist who was ready to shoot hostile Arabs. I asked him, "Suppose you had been born an Arab, what would be your ideal?" He laughed, embarrassed, realizing that if his mother had conceived him by a different man, he might have killed Jews. What is the value of an ideal that depends on the circumstance of partners in the sexual act?

I was acquainted with a young lady who had not known her father and presumed he was an Indian. In her youth her heart glowed for India's fight for independence. She was unable to agree with Gandhi that it should proceed at his slow pace. It had to be achieved immediately, even at the cost of shedding British blood. Then she found out that her father had actually been a Jew. From that moment she became a Zionist fighter.

Isn't this tragic? But isn't it the history of each one of us? Should not some of the impressive personalities of the liberation movements take themselves less seriously? They are ready to shed blood for an ideal, not because after calm reflection they have decided it is the highest, but just because they were born on one side of a border or social pyramid instead of the other.

We agree with terrorists in their readiness to sacrifice themselves for the highest cause they know. The Latins had a proverb: *Dolce et decorum est pro patria mori*—"It is sweet and beautiful to die for the fatherland." The same can be said of other high ideals.

Let us never think about terrorists as just killers, ignoring the fact that they are also ready to suffer in jail and even to die for the cause they serve. We are united with them in hatred for unjust structures. It is wrong for one nation to oppress another. Those who fight against this are right. It is wrong for privileged nations, races, or classes to exist at the expense of others. It is wrong to be a dictator and amass great wealth while others suffer. It is also wrong to slaughter embryos indiscriminately. Terror against unborn children and the killing of abortionists are also wrong.

Lenin started the Russian Communist revolution, and as a result tens of millions of innocent people died. He had no scruples about sentencing not only individuals but whole categories of people to death—because he claimed to want a better future for mankind. It was said that "he loved mankind so much that he was ready to kill all men for the benefit of humanity."

Lenin's older brother had been hanged for his attempt to kill the Russian emperor. Lenin shared his brother's ideal to get rid of oppressors, but he thought that individual acts of terror would not achieve this end. He says in his writings that a party of well-trained professional revolutionaries have to seize power in the state. These will kill their opponents wholesale, after which, in time, the happy Socialist society will arise. He died disillusioned.

Stalin had been a terrorist. Together with a few comrades he attacked a big transport of state money en route from one bank to another and plundered it. He took not one cent for himself but gave all he had stolen to the Communist party, then called Bolsheviks, to be used for revolutionary purposes. He was thrown in jail and deported for twelve years. He suffered for what he considered right. His purpose had been to do good to the poor and downtrodden people. We share this sentiment.

Stalin was not totally wrong, nor are any of the terrorists. The tragedy is that, when he later came to power, he jailed and killed wholesale not only the rich exploiters and tyrants but also millions of peasants in order to collectivize agriculture. He also killed his own comrades, those with whom he had previously fought and suffered. He even killed his own family.

Hitler had no selfish motives. He really loved the German nation, though he himself was Austrian. For the good of the fatherland he was ready to kill millions of Jews, gypsies, and people of other nations he considered a hindrance to

Germany's progress. He killed even German dissidents. He loved—but with what limited love!

There was something terribly amiss about these characters, as well as other terrorists who participated in crimes though not to such a horrendous extent. We cannot say that they were totally wrong. The point of departure—the desire to help the poor and downtrodden—was right.

I cannot totally reject a Muslim terrorist either. He kills, but he also sacrifices his own life with the shout *Allahu akbar!*—"God is great!" In my homeland of Romania, Fascist terrorists called "legionnaires" were fanatical Orthodox Christians. Before killing the prime minister, Calinescu, they spent a whole night stretched out on the floor of a church praying that God might bless their endeavor. Their zeal for God was commendable. What they knew about God and His will was insufficient.

Take Time for Reflection

TERRORISTS are wrong in being led by passion. They do not meditate thoroughly about their ways.

In Hebrew, one of the languages of the Bible, the word for "to think" is *lekhshov*. The root of this word, *kheshbon*, reveals that in the Hebrew mentality "to think" means "to calculate." In all major aspects of life, we have to calculate the possible profits or losses resulting from an action. Jesus asks men, "What does it *profit* to gain the whole world and lose your own soul?" (Mark 8:36).

The prophet Isaiah writes, "God teaches you to profit" (Isaiah 48:17), not in the ugly sense of exploiting poverty and ignorance, but in order to engage in activities that lead to a noble aim. Anyone inclined toward terrorist acts should calculate the chances of success, learning from the history of terrorism. By the same token, he should calculate whether the overthrow of an unjust structure would lead to a better one.

The Nazis used terror. Hitler summarized their intent by saying they were building a "thousand-year empire." His "empire" lasted a mere fifteen years and left Germany in shambles. It was the same with Italian fascism. In Russia, communism had as its predecessor the terrorist organization *Narodnaya Volya* (The People's Will). This began what the Communists practiced for decades: terrorist attacks against the royal family and political leaders. The Communists succeeded in gaining power, which they retained for seventy years, even exporting it to many other countries.

The result? The Russian Empire is a basket case. Socialism appears to have been only a mirage. Communism deprived a whole nation of liberty. The people are now far poorer than in capitalist countries. Was it worthwhile for the terrorists to give their blood and shed the blood of others? Did they serve the people?

Yugoslavia has experienced decades of terrorism. Serbian terrorists killed the Austrian Prince Ferdinand. A Croatian killed the Serbian King Alexander I. These are only the most illustrious victims. The Communist Tito and the Fascist Ustashi killed wholesale. Yugoslavia is in ruins.

The intentions of the terrorists might have been right, but isn't it time to learn from the past that terror does not pay?

How much terror had been exercised in the violent French Revolution, which overthrew the monarchy in 1789 with the slogan "Liberty, equality, fraternity"? After the bloody Reign of Terror, the revolutionists celebrated their victory under this banner. Do equality and fraternity reign in France?

In the nineteenth century, France expanded its hegemony over vast African and Asian territories and became an empire by oppressing the

indigenous peoples. From among these, terrorist groups arose and succeeded. In our century,
French power was overthrown on both continents. Algeria was freed, but Islamic fundamen-
talist terrorists arose against the new Algerian
government and then were hanged without any
mercy. Likewise, in Egypt, revolutionists overthrew King Farouk. Now a democratic republic,
Egypt has produced a new type of revolutionist
adversary. These too are hanged. If they came to
power, they would hang others.

The Vietnamese fought to free themselves
from France, after which followed a cruel Communist dictatorship. Now their government is
begging for help from capitalists.

But haven't there been useful armed fights
against injustice? Who can say? Perhaps American independence could have been attained
without war. Almost all British colonies and
those of other empires obtained their freedom
without war and its destruction. King George II,
against whose injustice the American colonists
rebelled, did not live forever. Perhaps under
another king the immediate cause of the rebellion would have disappeared and the painful
separation between two English-speaking peoples could have been avoided.

America's war of secession was not absolutely necessary. Slavery had been abolished in
the British Empire without the shedding of
blood.

For the same reason, it is questionable if armed fighting of governments against terrorists will make them disappear.

Enlarge Your Love

TERRORISTS are idealists, usually with beautiful concepts of liberty, justice, a readiness for self-sacrifice, a willingness to go to the uttermost in the service of what they consider a worthy cause, and also loyalty, measured by the severe punishment they mete out to disloyal comrades.

We are wrong to think there is little love in the world. Tigers kill to provide food for their cubs. I knew a man who killed for money to buy his little son a costly toy the boy had seen in a shop window. The father was poor and could not bear the tears of his child, who knew other boys received toys from their fathers. This man committed a crime prompted by love.

Tigers and men (even the worst) have some love, however instinctive or misguided, for their young. There is love in the world. But it needs to be enlarged to embrace wider spheres and to be channeled toward better causes. Wolves kill men; dogs defend men to the death. Yet both wolves and dogs have common ancestors.

God enabled me to bring to Christ a massmurderer who, during World War II, had killed many Jews, even children, and boasted of what he had done. He had been told that Jews were a threat to his fatherland, which he loved. God gave him the grace to see that love limited to one's fatherland can be enlarged. It can comprehend men of other nations and other social groups. Later I had written proof that this criminal became a savior of men, saving the lives of many who were condemned to death.

In the thirties, Germany had a Jewish secretary of state. A young fanatical German nationalist, unable to bear the shame that a Jew should be a government official, shot him. Mrs. Rathenau, a Christian, visited the murderer in jail and taught him to enlarge his love to include all men because all are creatures of the same God. During World War II, this murderer became a high-ranking officer in the German army stationed in Marseille, France and used his position to save many Jews from death. The Nazis discovered this and hanged him. He died for the right cause—a superior love. Everyone desires higher positions, greater revenues, more influential friendships. Why not a higher quality of love?

Love is a better counselor than hatred. William Wilberforce achieved his goal of abolishing slavery in the British Empire without shedding one drop of blood. He did so with loving words. Mahatma Gandhi was appalled at the injustice Indians suffered under British rule. He obtained his country's liberty through *ahimsa*, nonviolence. His adherents did not commit any acts of violence.

When Gandhi's ideal—freedom from British rule—had been achieved, millions of innocents died in violent fights between Hindus and

Muslims. Instead of the one free country Gandhi dreamt of, there are now three: India, Pakistan, and Bangladesh, which are at loggerheads with one another. Was the fight worthwhile?

When a white racist attacked the black American Baptist pastor Martin Luther King as he was preaching, members of the congregation quickly leaped to his defense. But King deflected them, saying, "If I had been educated like this man, I would also have acted like him. Understand and forgive him! Let him go."

In 1917, there was a prolonged battle at the river Isonzo between Austrian and Italian troops. It was a battle of position. For many months the warring troops fought from trenches only a few yards apart. At Christmas a group of Austrian soldiers, wishing to mock the enemy, filled a soldier's boot with dirt, wrapped it nicely like a gift, then had a powerful man hurl it directly into the Italian trench. Some Christians among the Italians decided to reciprocate. After washing the boot thoroughly, they filled it with oranges and candy, wrapped it, and threw it back to the Austrian trench. When the soldiers there unwrapped it, they found a brief message that read, "Everyone gives what he has."

Since some oppress others and commit injustice, should we act at their low level? Can't we do better?

Though Christians comprise less than one percent of Japan's population, it was a Christian who organized their trade union movement:

Toyohiko Kagawa. He taught workers to obtain their rights while avoiding violent conflict. The Japanese were not aware of massive strikes and lockouts in other industrial countries.

At a certain point, a large manufacturing company decided to lower salaries. Some workers, revolted by this injustice, proposed a violent reaction—a strike—which would have paralyzed the factories. "Don't do it," Kagawa advised. "Rather, send a delegation to the president of the company, bow politely before him, and say, 'We regret that we were so heartless as not to realize the difficulties through which you are passing. Our children are used to deprivations, while yours aren't. We will gladly work for you without taking any salary just to show you our faithfulness to the enterprise.'"

They accepted no further salary, but in the evening workers would station themselves on Tokyo's great boulevards carrying baskets with a large inscription: "Give for our poor company," which they named. They also explained matters to passers-by, thus engaging the sympathy of the public.

No longer were salaries lowered; rather, they were increased.

On the other hand, Kagawa organized a strike of the employees on trams. However, they continued to run the trams regularly so as not to paralyze the life of a big city. The only difference was that they refused to collect the fare, allowing people to ride free of charge. In the end, this original kind of strike was successful. Love and goodness are not doomed to failure. They can win.

In South Africa, apartheid—which made nonwhites second-class citizens—has been abolished, but not as a result of an armed fight, terrorist acts, or rebellion, which had proved ineffective. Apartheid bowed to pressure applied by the Western powers, mobilized by a wave of sympathy on the part of those who favored racial justice.

One thought would restrain me from committing violent acts: the one I injure is my brother. He may not suffer like me, but he has his own sufferings. There exists much pain among the ruling classes of a nation. Proof of this is the fact that depression and suicide are as frequent among the rich as among the poor. I have known well a multitude of men on both sides of the social spectrum: on the whole, one class is no happier than the other.

Among Christians are adherents of what is called Liberation Theology. This philosophy originated within the Catholic Church and extended into the Protestant camp belonging to the World Council of Churches (WCC). They went very far by providing support to many terrorists in the armed fight. Some priests were even known to set aside Bibles for guns.

The Liberationists did not consider those they helped "terrorists" but "freedom fighters." I too don't like to call people by names they abhor. It is all right to call them freedom fighters if you make it clear that they fight heroically for their concept of how they think freedom can be attained. Others, just as well-intentioned as these freedom fighters, think otherwise. Catholics used to call Protestants "heretics." Now they say "separated brethren," which is much nicer. William Shakespeare wrote, "That which we call a rose by any other name would smell as sweet."

However, the adherents of Liberation Theology showed a bias that excluded truth. They supported only leftist fighters against tyrannies, ignoring the millions of innocents who were killed at the same time by Communist regimes. Russian, Romanian, and similar newspapers now reveal this about governments that recently have fallen from power. The U.S. also supported guerrilla movements, but only those that suited their interests. South African governments supported such movements in Mozambique and Angola that fought against communism to the exclusion of others.

As a well-motivated "freedom fighter" willing to shed blood for a noble cause, are you also willing to be used as a pawn by others not honest in their intentions? Ponder this.

One of the most violent terrorist groups in the world is the Irish Republican Army (IRA). It is composed of Catholics who fight to have Northern Ireland, which is now under the British Crown, reunited with Ireland. But the English and the Irish speak the same language and share the same culture. The old Irish language is virtually obsolete. English is the language spoken in the Irish parliament, government, and universities. The religious cleavage also belongs to the past. Church attendance is very low in both countries, and the respective religions are mostly hereditary.

In the South, Catholics and Protestants get along well. There is not the slightest discrimination. Why should the Northerners be adamantly opposed to uniting with the South? Why should the Southern terrorists be just as determined that the North leave the British Empire?

This fight, like so many other battles between humans, has no reasonable motives. The reasons invoked by each side are rationalizations arising from the impulse to rebel for rebellion's sake. The ideal proclaimed is a pretext.

Is Terrorism a Universal Remedy?

DO TERRORISTS think about the effect their fight will have on the social group to which they belong?

In Romania, three Jewish Communists—Goldstein, Osias, and Lichtblau—placed a bomb in the Senate. Two men died and others were wounded. In Bulgaria, a terrorist group led by a Jewish Communist named Friedman put a bomb in the cathedral of Sofia. Many died. A Jew, Grunspan, killed a German diplomat in Paris in Nazi times. The result was a strengthening of anti-Semitism, which is also completely unreasonable. In Germany, the result of the one killing of a diplomat was what was called "the crystal night." All Jews had to pay a fine of one billion marks. Jewish properties were confiscated and destroyed. Uncounted Jews were put in concentration camps where many died.

The Latins used to pose the question, *Cui prodest?*—"Who profits?" Surely not the cause for which terrorists stand.

When Arabs plotted terrorist acts in the U.S., anti-Arab sentiment arose among Americans. The terrorists are Muslims, but the resentment extends beyond Muslim Arabs to include Christian Arabs. They too are shunned.

Around the globe there are countless terrorist movements with widely divergent and even contradictory aims. With such diversity, can terrorism be a universal panacea able to cure all social ills of whatever stripe? Consider just a few: The African National Council (ANC), fighting apartheid in South Africa; the opposition of white Afrikaaners to the abolition of apartheid; the IRA, fighting to incorporate Northern Ireland into the Irish Republic; Protestant terrorists in northern Ireland who kill IRA members; the Palestine Liberation Organization (PLO) and Hamas (whose slogan is "Only a dead Jew is a good Jew"), which planned the destruction of the State of Israel; the fanatical Zionist organization "Kach," whose aim is to drive all Arabs from Israel; the "Opposition of White Aryans," fighting to deprive American Blacks and Asians of their rights; the Communist organization "Sendero Luminoso" (Shining Path) in Peru, which kills recklessly; "Tupamaros," active in several Latin American countries; the Islamic organizations Hezb Islami, Jamiat Islami, and Ettchad Islami, which fought in Afghanistan against their former comrades in arms who have come to power in the capital of Kabul; Kamredine Kherbane fighting in Algeria for the introduction of Sharia, the Islamic law (members of this organization are often hanged by the government); Jamiat Islami and Hizbul Mujahideen in Kashmir (India), as well as the organization of rebellious Sikhs in Punjab (India); Islamic Liberation

Front of Ormya in Ethiopia; Abou Sayaf in the Philippines; All-Ittihad-al-Islami in Somalia; the Party of Islamic Renewal and that of Islamic Resistance in Tadjikistan; the Khmer Rouge in Cambodia; the ETA, Basque terrorists fighting the Spanish government. I could go on and on.

Would you have confidence in a medical school that offered one pill to cure tuberculosis, syphilis, malaria, stroke, and toothache? It is just as unreasonable to believe that one method— killing all adversaries or overthrowing them from power—will cure all social ills.

What Will You Think About Your Deeds After Committing Them?

ALL SUCH organizations fight for power without considering that the possession of power is useful only if one has the capacity to rule a nation. Lenin once wrote that "under communism a cook will be able to rule a country." As a result, under communism men without a knowledge of politics, economics, and social problems ruled a huge state. The result was predictable: the bankruptcy of Communist governments in the whole of Eastern Europe. Similarly, nazism and fascism led to the ruin of Germany and Italy at the end of World War II.

Terrorism starts with a limited purpose—but who is master of his will? Tempted by increasing power, who sticks to his original intent? Political and religious power is addictive, like gambling. Many gamblers can't stop until they have lost everything. Terrorists begin by aiming at certain individuals or categories of men they consider dangerous to their cause, but soon they degenerate.

Racist terrorists desecrate Jewish cemeteries. In Yugoslavia there have been directed attacks against cultural objects. South African terrorists entered a church and shot worshipers indiscriminately during a religious service. Why did they pick a church, and why did they decide to kill victims as they worshiped? One man of the organization "Kach" shot Muslims while they prayed in a mosque in Israel. So often terrorism resorts to acts that no longer correspond to its primary purpose.

When you think about defining your ideals and the methods for achieving them (the details of some terrorist acts are elaborated with remarkable efficiency), evaluate your thinking. What kind of mind do you have? The Romanian word for "mind" is the same as the one for "to lie." The mind can be a liar. The mind calculates all of your attitudes, but how good a calculator is your mind? Consider only the fact that the mind can fool us in some of our dreams. Then why always trust it when you are awake?

Terrorists do not practice self-criticism. They are absolutely sure they are right. Without this conviction they could not kill. But at a certain time they thought otherwise, never planning to kill or even having a revulsion to killing. How will they feel after their first murder—or the tenth?

Fyodor Dostoyevsky, the renowned Russian writer, was a terrorist in his youth. He and a few comrades were sentenced to die. While waiting his turn, he looked down at the crowd that had assembled to enjoy the spectacle and realized the vanity of the aim he had set for himself. He had desired to help free these people, but they did not wish to be helped or freed by him. They preferred the macabre amusement of watching him die, knowing they too would someday die. All his grandiose plans and futile endeavors for his brief life now seemed plain stupid. Doesn't religion speak about eternal life? If indeed it exists, would it not be much more important than being concerned about the merits of monarchy, democracy, or socialism?

This was the beginning of Dostoyevsky's conversion. Just before he was executed, his sentence was commuted to four years in a labor camp. Once freed, he became one of Russia's most important Christian writers.

No individual knows what he will think the very next day. Since this is true, should I kill today when I may spend the rest of my life regretting what I have done? By way of contrast, Christian martyrs say with the apostle Paul, "I am nothing" (1 Corinthians 13:2). He also writes that all true Christians "are nothing" (Galatians 6:3). Christ requires that Christians deny themselves so that He may live in them and direct every step of their life. Christians walk with secure steps. Even when they do something very different from what they previously thought, they are at peace. Yesterday was ordered by the same One who orders today. It was a preparation.

The elementary, childish things you are taught in school in the first grade are not wrong. At that stage of development, they are the right thing. First a child learns the alphabet, then he is taught to write words, then sentences. So it is with other matters in life.

Our lives as Christians are governed by the One who created life; therefore, we can be serene, without the terrible crises of unbelievers. We know God's love to be the thread that ties together the events of our lives like a string of pearls.

The Positive Side of Terrorism

THERE IS not only a negative side to terrorists, but also a positive. There is a basis on which we can try to build friendship, if only they will agree to enlarge their capacity for love and loyalty. A man can do better than to love just one race, one party, one nation, one culture, one class, one ideology. So we say to you, our terrorist friends, don't keep to your narrow loves and loyalties. Enlarge them, expand them.

We appreciate the fact that, since you are ready to suffer greatly for an ideal, you have freed yourselves from much selfishness.

One song often sung in churches is "Hosanna [in Hebrew, "Save, please"] in the highest." We urge you to aim for the highest. Allow yourselves to be saved in the highest sense of the word. Grasp the all-embracing love, and all-embracing ideals of God, which should multiply what Jesus did two thousand years ago. The Christian ideal lies beyond what was expressed in the limited Hebrew language during His earthly life.

Paul said, "You are a new creation" (2 Corinthians 5:17), just as you would say to a caterpillar, "You are not meant to crawl on the ground; you are called to be a beautiful, multicolored butterfly that flits from flower to flower giving joy to

children." You have the possibility of overcom-
ing sin, temptation, all human pettiness. You
have the possibility of sitting with Jesus and His
Father, the supreme God, on His throne to reign
with Him (Revelation 3:21).

We admire you for your readiness to sacrifice
yourselves; but don't do it in the service of too
narrow a cause. Jesus offers you an ideal worthy
of this supreme sacrifice: life eternal.

Side-Effects
of Terrorism

RIGHT JUDGMENT demands an analysis of all the aspects of an action, without neglecting any. A terrorist act is planned. It will kill an important enemy. But this enemy has innocent children or an old mother whose heart may break. Have you taken this into consideration?

In Dostoyevsky's novel *Crime and Punishment*, we are told about a poor student who could not bear the thought that his sister was ready to give herself to a disgusting old rich man only to enable her brother to continue his studies. He knew an old lady who lived by letting students pawn their little valuables for small loans. She knew they would not be able to pay back the money plus the enormous interest she charged, so the precious objects would remain hers.

He asked himself, "What good is it that such a bedbug should live? She serves no one. She only does harm. If I kill her and take her money, I can save my virtuous sister from prostituting herself."

He thought about every detail of the murder he would commit and was satisfied. He could not fail. But just as he was killing her, the old woman's sister, generally known to be a good Christian, entered the room. To keep her from denouncing him, he had to kill her too.

A newly discovered medicine might cure an illness but might also have dangerous side-effects. Do you think about all the side-effects of a terrorist act?

In many countries under a dictatorship and in the third world, when terrorists are caught, the whole family goes to jail. Do you ever think about how your mother weeps to know you're a terrorist, to know you're in jail or sentenced to death, or even executed? Is it right to expose to such an ordeal the one who gave you birth and nursed you as an infant?

Terrorist friends! Just think of your mothers. What pain and irreparable harm you cause them. Is it right to do so? Should mothers be made to weep?

Libyan terrorists blew up a plane over Lockerbie, Scotland, causing the death of a hundred innocent people. What was their guilt and what good resulted for the cause of the terrorists? In Lebanon, 220 U.S. marines were killed in a car-bomb explosion. What guilt did these men bear, and what did the cause of Palestinian liberty win by this act?

And what is the end result of terror? Look at the many countries recently freed from communism. The Communists used terror to gain power, then used terror to "liberate" the population from poverty. Contrary to all promises and expectations, the population became poorer, not richer. Only a very small percentage profited from the revolution. In Russia, Stalin jailed or shot all the former terrorists who had somehow escaped the Czar's gallows. In the end, communism collapsed.

While we as Christians do not agree with much of the terrorists' agenda, can we look upon them with less than love? They are the natural product of the society we have built. On American television programs for children, 32 acts of violence are shown per hour. By the time a child is twelve, he has viewed 18,000 murders. What results could such an education give? We instilled in the younger generation the spirit of destruction. We reap what we have sown. Some of them find delight in setting forest fires, others in wanton murder. Such things happen in the U.S. as well as in Mediterranean lands.

In some American and Western newspapers, Fidel Castro and Mao Tse-tung have been hailed as valuable reformers. Mao taught that "power lies in the barrel of a gun."

Think Now About What You Will Say on Your Deathbed

DEAR TERRORIST friends, we tell you frankly that we have no illusions. We know that the chances of convincing you to forgo your ways and become disciples of love are very slim. But perhaps you will have a moment of illumination.

Andropov succeeded Brezhnev as dictator of the USSR. As a young officer of the Secret Police, Andropov was once confronted with the prisoner Nikolai Hrapov, a Christian pastor, for interrogation.

Hrapov argued his case with the dictator: "I have read atheist books; I suppose you must have read Christian books. Can you tell me what is wrong about our convictions?"

Andropov with a smile—it is said he always smiled—put a bullet in his revolver and told Hrapov, "You see, a bullet costs only fifty cents. This is enough to overthrow all the proofs you have that God exists."

Such men who worship violence exclude themselves from the realm of reason. But we rely on the fact that they cannot forgo reason totally. Andropov left a notebook at his death in which he had written, "The world existed millions of years without me. I have lived a very short while. Soon I will die. And the world will continue to exist for more millions of years. I will be completely forgotten. It is terrible to think about this."

Atheists too have moments of light, if not earlier, then on their deathbed. We rely on miracles. We believe that our weak challenge will be heeded by the best and wisest of you.

Andropov had not been a fool to trust in the power of bullets. Almost all those who instigated the Russian Revolution of 1917 were shot by their own comrade Stalin. Even more, they consented to declare at public trials, after being tortured by their own comrades in the Secret Police and threatened with guns that had bullets in their barrels, that they had never been revolutionists but agents of Western imperialism. They believed the promise that they would escape the death sentence if they gave this testimony. The promise was not kept.

After this, all heads of the Soviet Secret Police were arrested by Stalin and tortured—Yagoda, Ezhov, Beria. They also confessed in public that they had never been true Communists but spies of capitalists. Together with them thousands of officers of their Secret Police were killed by the same Secret Police.

Was the fight of Russian terrorists to overthrow the unjust czarist regime worthwhile if what followed—the cruel Soviet regime—was the result? Should one escape from a bear only to be torn by a lion?

My heart breaks thinking about the many terrorists hanged in such countries as Algeria, Egypt, and Iran, and about the tortures they must have endured in some countries before their execution.

Are states unable to find another way to handle their young citizens who have gone astray?

Look at those who are hanged. The great majority of terrorists come from the poorer class. They have known unemployment, hunger, despair. Those of the wealthier classes had no moral education in schools and no examples of morality in public life. In school I learned trigonometry and Latin, which I never had to use. I never learned what life was all about, what my duties were and where I could obtain the spiritual power to fulfill them.

I have shown you, my terrorist friends, that I have understanding for you. Until now we have reasoned. But is reason alone enough to give us truth and guide us in life? Reason helps us sort out and react rightly to the realities of our life in the world we know. But what part of the world do we know? And how much do we know about the world we do know?

Astronomy tells us that there are millions of galaxies containing countless billions of stars. Our sun is one of them in a corner of one medium-size galaxy. This is the macrocosm. What and who is in these galaxies and beyond them?

But there is also the microcosm, composed of trillions of elementary particles in constant movement, colliding with each other, with a lifespan of a billionth of a second! As they disappear, others are formed. There is not one cubic inch of matter that is not the theater of such clashes between elementary particles.

Is there any sense in the tremendous events that take place in the macrocosm and microcosm?

We live on the earth, a speck of dust in an infinite universe or perhaps multiverse. Who knows? Much of the universe is constituted of what astronomers call dark matter. We know it exists because it exercises attractions that we can measure, but it does not give signals that make it perceptible. What is happening in that arena?

We live in a world that turns on its axis and revolves around the sun, then moves with the whole solar system around the galaxy center, and finally moves with our galaxy through space.

The rotation of the earth sometimes experiences sudden stops or slowdowns. You have never sensed it. Perhaps there are some other very important things that you do not sense.

In addition to the material universe, there is also the universe of thoughts, sentiments, emotions, passions, desires, aspirations, hopes, inclinations. There are not only jails and gallows where men suffer and die. There is also the hell of remorse, guilt, fear, and anxiety; the fixation on the retina of scenes of horror either endured or perpetrated; the nightmares of evildoers whose sins have never been discovered by society; horrible sufferings in dreams, described by the prophet Daniel (chapter 7).

Therefore the political and economic changes envisioned by terrorists are not sufficient because they don't address the inner man, the burdened conscience. They don't take into account the unconscious, the subconscious, and the superconscious aspects of a man's being. There are intuitions, not learned, of things you never perceived. There exist high ideals. Where do they come from? Are they from our material structure?

I know I have lungs although I have never seen them. The fact that I breathe is proof enough for me that I have lungs. Sometimes thoughts occur to me that did not originate solely within my brain. I feel an ardent love for ideals that surprise me in their ability to inflame me when usually I am entirely otherwise than the ideal Richard Wurmbrand I wish to realize. Why?

If breathing is proof enough that I have lungs, these high thoughts—like the thoughts of terrorists to sacrifice themselves for what they consider a noble cause—indicate that there must be a higher intelligence and a higher love that inspires them, even if dimly perceived. In English, we believe that the source of all that is most beautiful, right, good, and loving is "God"—this word evokes in our minds a mighty and benevolent person.

Whatever image you have of the source of all power, there is surely a supreme Being who created, rules, and has put in us tremendous possibilities to be grand for all eternity ourselves.

The Justification of Unbelief

I DO NOT HOLD it against you, my terrorist friends, that you do not entrust your life to God or to His messenger Jesus. I realize that it may be difficult for you to believe in a supernatural Being.

The story is told of a Chinese gentleman who sat in his home quietly sipping his tea. A knock came at the door. It was the police.

"You are sentenced to twenty lashes. Quick! Bare yourself and stretch out to receive them."

He did so, and the police left. Then he returned to the table to finish his tea. He knew he lived under a dictatorship where this was a common occurrence.

The next day, as he sat at the breakfast table, again someone knocked at the door. Again it was the police. "You are sentenced to receive twenty lashes."

Without uttering a word, he bared himself and received them. On the third day the ritual was repeated. On the fourth day again there was a knock at the door as he drank his tea. Baring himself, he called, "Enter."

Instead of the police, beloved friends walked in. "Have you also come to beat me?" he asked, unable to believe that people could come to his house with good intentions.

So many have lied to us and led us astray that we have come to the point where we can't even believe God. Our total capacity to believe has been thwarted. God does not complain. He is not the only one who is not believed. We no longer believe in the stranger who knocks at our door.

Nazi terrorists were lied to by Hitler, who had promised a thousand-year Aryan Empire. Communist leaders promised an earthly paradise—another lie. So many comrades of the terrorists proved to be agents of the Secret Police infiltrated into their ranks. Even parents, children, and spouses prove to be denouncers. For terrorists it is simply difficult to believe unknown persons. No wonder they cannot believe God.

How Is It That
Belief Exists?

TERRORISTS surely do well to count on the
fact that people are often unreliable. That
being so, why in the world do we have within us
the ability to believe and to trust? We must find
it useful. We have the ability to breathe, to smell,
to taste, to think, to work, because these are
useful activities. Why the ability to believe?

We have hands because they are needed for
work. We have feet because they are needed for
transport. We have the ability to believe and to
trust because there is One worthy of being
trusted and believed in: God, the all-loving Creator. It is God who revealed to us the sense of life.
Through all His prophets and through Jesus, He
revealed that this topsy-turvy world, whose injus-
tices you do well to hate, is not the whole world.
It is the preparatory stage for a world of truth,
justice, light, love, and joy.

What good are the puzzles you find in maga-
zines? They stimulate your mind to find a solution. What good are obstacle races? They
challenge you to develop your athletic skills. Just
so, the intricate world into which we have been
born has stimulated the human mind to create
and develop in the arts and sciences. As a result,
we now have fast travel by land, sea, and air;
amplified hearing through microphones, hear-

ing aids, stereo systems; extended vision through space telescopes, electronic microscopes, and X-rays.

Why do we have such brains and such minds? What need was there for mankind to have a brain that would search out distant galaxies and explore the past looking for a beginning of the universe? What need was there for a Shakespeare or a Beethoven? A simple "human organism" would have fared well without compositions.

We have a higher calling that tells about another world.

Suppose an unborn child could think. Doubtless it would regard as "stupid religion" the idea that it would eventually have a life outside the womb. Can a child conceive of what awaits him as an adult? I am now 85. In my youth I knew thousands of old people, but it was beyond me to understand the life and thinking of an old man. So we cannot imagine our next stage as being in eternity.

Now supposing a child in the womb could think rationally, it might ask, "How come I have eyes? I live in complete darkness. Am I being prepared for another existence where there is light and color? Why do I have legs? They embarrass me. Since I can't even stretch them out, might they serve me in another world where I will have to walk or run? What good are my arms and hands? They crowd my body uselessly. Perhaps someday I will need them to work, to grasp,

to build. Why do I need a tongue? I cannot speak
or eat. This too must serve a future purpose."

But adults are in the same predicament. Just
when they have accumulated knowledge, wisdom, and experience in life, the hearse awaits
them. It would seem that all is in vain. But just as
the embryo has a sequel, even so our earthly life
has a sequel: eternal life, life after death.

Every seven years all the cells in my body are
replaced. By the age of 85, I have exchanged all
my cells twelve times. Only nerve cells are per-
manent, but they too have a metabolism. The
molecules of which they are constituted change
continually. I can say, without the slightest ex-
ception, that I have not one molecule left of
those I had seven years ago, and at that time I
had none of those I had fourteen years ago.

Who is the "I" who had these different bod-
ies that are replaced continually? One cannot
bathe twice in the same river. The water you see
in it today is not the same you saw yesterday.
Likewise I am not the same entity I was yesterday.
I am in a process of becoming. Becoming what?

People believe that man is a body that has a
soul. The inverse is the truth: we are eternal souls
that during their earthly life don different bod-
ies, from that of an embryo to that of an old man.

Our mental structure also changes con-
stantly. Do you still think like a child or a lad of
fourteen? Do you have the same affections? Do
you like or dislike the same persons, books,
games, food? Then who is the "I" who changes

your mentality? Has anybody ever seen this mysterious "I" dying?

Man needs very few basic things to be fully satisfied: food, clothing, housing, health, some possibility of intellectual preoccupations, little pleasures, and a sexual partner. Yet there have been millionaires with access to all these things who committed suicide. The cause: deep depression. What depressed them, since they had everything a person could need or desire? The soul that inhabits the earthly body.

On the other hand, when I was in jail with men imprisoned for their convictions, I saw them sing though they were beaten, hungry, trembling with cold, separated from all they loved, with no books. What caused them to be happy? Their soul.

The amazing thing is that the soul can be independent of external circumstances and events. It can remain unaffected by death, which is an advancement to a higher sphere where earthly quarrels seem like child's play.

The Challenge of Evil in the World

ALL THE EVILS you see in this life are challenges. Everything that is wrong in the world—and it is much—should be a calling not to become angry but to do better than others. The apostle Paul wrote, "Run so as to get the prize" (1 Corinthians 9:24). In a world of hate, injustice, and greed, be an example of love, mercy, and goodness! Among the haughty, shine with the power of good character, while at the same time exhibiting modesty. Be the servant of all! This is the secret of real power.

Hear what Jesus said about the ideal life to lead:

"You have heard that it was said to those of old, 'You shall not murder,' and whoever murders will be in danger of the judgment. But I say to you that whoever is angry with his brother without a cause shall be in danger of the judgment. And whoever says to his brother, 'Idiot!' shall be in danger of the council. But whoever says, 'You fool!' shall be in danger of hell fire.

"Therefore if you bring your gift to the altar, and there remember that your brother has something against you, leave your gift there before the altar, and go your way. First be reconciled to your brother, and then come and offer your gift.

"Agree with your adversary quickly, while you are on the way with him, lest your adversary deliver you to the judge, the judge hand you over to the officer, and you are thrown into prison."

"I tell you not to resist an evil person. But whoever slaps you on your right cheek, turn the other to him also.

"If anyone wants to sue you and take away your tunic, let him have your cloak also. And whoever compels you to go one mile, go with him two. Give to him who asks you, and from him who wants to borrow from you do not turn away.

"You have heard that it was said, 'You shall love your neighbor and hate your enemy.' But I say to you, love your enemies, bless those who curse you, do good to those who hate you, and pray for those who spitefully use you and persecute you, that you may be sons of your Father in heaven; for He makes His sun rise on the evil and on the good, and sends rain on the just and on the unjust.

"For if you love those who love you, what reward have you? Do not even the tax collectors do the same? And if you greet your brethren only, what do you do more than others? Do not even the tax collectors do so? Therefore you shall be perfect, just as your Father in heaven is perfect."

"Do not lay up for yourselves treasures on earth, where moth and rust destroy and where thieves break in and steal; but lay up for yourselves treasure in heaven, where neither moth nor rust destroys and where thieves do not break in and steal. For where your treasure is, there your heart will be also.

"Why do you worry about clothing? Consider the lilies of the field, how they grow: they neither toil nor spin; and yet I say to you that even Solomon in all his glory was not arrayed like one of these.

"Now if God so clothes the grass of the field, which today is, and tomorrow is thrown into the oven, will He not much more clothe you, O you of little faith?

"Therefore do not worry, saying 'What shall we eat?' or 'What shall we drink?' or 'What shall we wear?' For after all these things the Gentiles seek. For your heavenly Father knows that you need all these things.

"But seek first the kingdom of God and His righteousness, and all these things shall be added to you. Therefore do not worry about tomorrow, for tomorrow will worry about its own things. Sufficient for the day is its own trouble.

"Judge not, that you be not judged. For with what judgment you judge, you will be judged; and with the same measure you use, it will be measured back to you.

"And why do you look at the speck in your brother's eye, but do not consider the plank in your own eye? Or how can you say to your brother, 'Let me remove the speck out of your eye'; and look, a plank is in your own eye? Hypocrite! First remove the plank from your own eye, and then you will see clearly to remove the speck out of your brother's eye."

"Therefore, whatever you want men to do to you, do also to them, for this is the Law and the Prophets."

Later the apostle Paul summarized some of Jesus' teachings:

"And though I bestow all my goods to feed the poor, and though I give my body to be burned, but have not love, it profits me nothing.

"Love suffers long and is kind; love does not envy; love does not parade itself, is not puffed up; does not behave rudely, does not seek its own, is not provoked, thinks no evil; does not rejoice in iniquity, but rejoices in the truth; bears all things, believes all things, hopes all things, endures all things."

What Happens After Death?

DURING THE period of harsh dictatorship in the former Soviet Union, I met an important person from its bureaucracy who wanted to talk politics. I replied, "I have something more important to say. I am an old man, and you too are advanced in age, though younger than I. One day I will no longer be a pastor and you will no longer represent your government, which opposes religion. One day we will both be dead.

"For a while, family and friends may come to put flowers on our graves. Then they too will die. We will be forgotten, as are most of the dead. We may lie undisturbed for a long time, but someday our graves may be plowed. It will be as if we had never been. What happens after death?"

Then I told him something about my life. I had been a sickly child. When I was very small, I overheard a doctor telling my mother, "This child cannot be cured. He will die." When he left, I asked Mother, "What does it mean to die?" She began to weep and left me without reply.

Soon after this my father died. At the funeral I saw Father lying in a coffin, then watched as the earth was shoveled over him. No Father any more? Will earth be shoveled over my corpse someday too?

In school, I was considered a good student and did well on my exams. But school did not really interest me. Why should I learn algebra, trigonometry, and Latin when I saw adults who never made use of them? The main subject that interested me was what happened after death.

I liked to take walks through cemeteries and read the tombstones. Highly valuable literature! I take such walks even now. One inscription says the person buried there was a general. There exists no higher rank. But he died. Another was a renowned millionaire. He died too. What happened to his millions? A third was a famous poet. He no longer enjoys the fame. Some were saints, others criminals; some revolutionists, others police officers who arrested them.

Later, when I was mature, I was shown the grave of the colonel of the Secret Police who had had me arrested, and I put a flower on it. If, as he believed, there is no life after death, he did not enjoy the flowers.

It seems that at death the curtain falls, and what had once been tragedy or comedy is ended. But in the theater, when the play is finished, the actor who died onstage arises and goes home. So it happens also at death.

I told the official that after many years of desiring an answer, I was given a Gospel. In it I read the story of One who had been, so to speak, thrice dead: first, crucified on a rude cross, then speared in the region of the heart, then immured in a rock-hewn tomb with a stone rolled against a door that was sealed and guarded by soldiers to make sure He stayed dead.

Did Jesus Arise from the Dead?

BUT THIS Man, Jesus the crucified, was resurrected on the third day. Unbelievable? So is our universe—except for the hard fact that it is there. This Man whose corpse was guarded by Roman soldiers met, walked, talked, and ate with His disciples.

This happened two thousand years ago. But down through the centuries thousands upon thousands of people in all walks of life have experienced His presence. You can too.

Consider impartially, as if you were on a jury, the following proofs of Jesus' resurrection:

What is the source of our knowledge of ancient history? The historians of their age, among them men like Homer, Herodotus, and Julius Caesar. What is the source of our knowledge of the activities of Jesus? Contemporary historians: their names are Matthew, Mark, Luke, John, Paul, and so on. Why should we believe some historians and not others?

Our intelligence should behave like an impartial court of law, carefully and competently weighing the statements of witnesses. In evaluating evidence we must consider not only what the witness says, but also his character and his trustworthiness. The credibility of the historians who described the life of Jesus is undoubtedly much greater than that of other historians. Who were the latter? Generally, they were paid to write by a royal personage, and their aim was not to make known the truth but rather to flatter their master, their people, or the social class to which they belonged.

By contrast, the historians who wrote the Gospels are of an entirely different stature. They risked loss of liberty and death for what they wrote. Matthew died as a martyr in Abyssinia, John was condemned to slave labor on the island of Patmos, and Paul was beheaded in Rome. Peter was crucified upside down.

No impartial court would lightly dismiss the evidence of witnesses ready to suffer such hardships for what they assert. All of them declare unanimously that they were convinced, by seeing, hearing, and touching, of the reality of Jesus' resurrection from the dead.

I know that this argument can be contradicted. What the other historians relate are things that can easily be understood and believed. They write about court intrigue, kings' favorites, plots, murder, war, things that happen even today, whereas the writers of the Gospels tell us of things that run counter to our human experience.

Among other things, they write of a virgin birth, of the healing of lepers by a simple touch, of walking on water, of the feeding of a great multitude with a few loaves, of men rising from the dead, and finally of Jesus' own resurrection, which was followed by His ascension into heaven. All these things come into the category of miracles, whereas today some "enlightened" people no longer believe in miracles.

The miracles that Jesus performed occurred in the sphere of the exceptional, whose existence cannot be denied. In everyday life it is not only ordinary things that occur. A man who does not believe in miracles is not a realist.

Furthermore, men consider as miracles things that a person with greater than average intelligence or muscular power can do and that a weak person with an ordinary intelligence is incapable of doing. Missionaries who have worked among primitive tribes record that the savages regard them as miracle-workers. This is not surprising since primitive people spend hours rubbing two pieces of wood together in order to produce a spark, whereas the missionary knows how to produce fire from a box of matches. He can even make stinking water burn. How is the savage to know that this "water" is gasoline?

The writer Pearl Buck informs us that when she told peasant women in backward parts of China that in England there were houses built on top of one another and that carriages moved through the streets without being drawn by horses, one of the women whispered, "What a lie! That sort of thing is impossible."

With sixty Spaniards under his command, Cortez conquered the powerful Aztec kingdom

because he appeared to the people he conquered to be a miracle-maker. In the first place,
the very appearance of the Spaniards was miraculous. Never before had the Aztecs seen white
men. Secondly, the newcomers possessed miraculous things that the Aztecs had never seen
before: horses and firearms. And so a huge kingdom fell without a struggle into the hands of a
few adventurers.

Jesus had a spiritual force such as no other
person has ever possessed. It is not surprising
that He was capable of performing miracles.
Being exceptional, He could do unique things
that would be impossible for ordinary men.

It is foolish to be prejudiced, declaring that
miracles are impossible and rejecting them without carefully examining the evidence of people
as trustworthy as the apostles. Either you can
believe in Jesus' miraculous resurrection from
the dead, or you have to believe in another
miracle that is still greater: that an effect exists
without a cause, because if Jesus did not arise
from the dead, the existence of the universal
Church would be such a miraculous happening.

Let's examine the evidence: Jesus wrote no
book, and while He lived on earth He did not
establish anything but a very small sect within
Judaism, a sect consisting mostly of unlearned
people who were not considered reputable citizens—sinful men, publicans, and fallen women.
Finally, one of His closest followers betrayed
Him, another denied Him, and the others de-

serted Him. He died on a cross, abandoned and apparently despairing, because as He hung on the cross He cried out, "My God, my God, why hast thou forsaken Me?"

After His death, He was buried, a large stone was placed in front of His sepulcher, and guards were posted. Meanwhile, His former disciples remained in hiding behind locked doors, and their only concern was to escape a death similar to that of their Master. This was how Jesus' life on earth ended. If He did not arise, how has the Christian Church come into being?

We have an explanation. On the third day, Jesus came back to life from the dead and appeared on numerous occasions to His apostles, assuring them that it was really Himself they saw, touched, and dined with. They came together again as they had previously, and the risen Jesus spent time instructing them, giving them guidance, and providing the power to do signs and wonders.

The very same cowardly Peter who had denied any knowledge of Jesus with curses and oaths stood up in the marketplace in Jerusalem and courageously testified that he had seen the risen Jesus. The other apostles did so too. Risking death, they traveled from one country to another, sealing with a martyr's death their conviction that Jesus had risen. In this way, the universal Church was born, it has grown, and it has survived, despite persecution and the unworthiness of its members.

If you are not prepared to admit that Jesus has risen from the dead, then this tremendous effect represented by the Christian Church—a Church that has survived for two thousand years and has millions of members—is an effect without a cause. It takes a greater naivete to accept the existence of such an effect without cause than to admit that Jesus Christ has really risen.

When a man enters a tall building, it might be a good idea, before climbing the stairs to the tenth floor, to go down first into the cellar and make sure that the foundations are sound. But why should it be necessary to do this? The fact that the building is standing is proof of the strength of the foundations.

The foundation stone on which the Christian Church was built is the resurrection of Jesus. The large, well-known building founded on this stone has stood for two millenniums and has resisted tremendous earthquakes. The existence of the Church is a proof that Christ has risen.

Another argument: Nowhere do we find that the enemies of the primitive Church at any time denied that the sepulcher of Jesus was found to be empty on Easter morning. It would have been quite natural for an investigation to be set on foot to discover whether the body had been stolen or desecrated. The reaction of the Jewish priests does not contradict the assertion that the grave was empty; they merely told the soldiers who had guarded the sepulcher to spread the rumor that His disciples had come during the night, while they were asleep, and stolen the body.

Now, if they were asleep, how could they have identified the thieves? Augustine rightly asks: "Does the synagogue introduce us to witnesses who were asleep when this deed was carried out?" If the Jewish priests really believed that Jesus' disciples had stolen the body, why were they not arrested, interrogated, and punished?

A strong movement must be carried forward by a strong impetus. The strong movement that has lasted for two thousand years and has had a worldwide effect, based on the belief in the resurrection of Jesus, cannot have been the product of hallucination. None of Jesus' disciples were men who suffered from hallucinations, certainly not doubting Thomas and the practical businessman Matthew, nor such men of the sea as Andrew, nor the cautious Nathaniel, nor Peter with his weak character. Only an event as tremendous as a real resurrection could have produced an impetus capable of starting a movement of this kind.

Nor must we forget that during the first thirty years after this event, most of Jesus' disciples suffered a violent death, and many of them were condemned to death precisely because they maintained that Jesus had risen from the dead. These things cannot have been invented.

Under the very noses of the Jewish priests, Jesus' apostles started to preach to the Jewish people, declaring that Jesus was the Messiah, a fact proved by His resurrection. In this way they came into conflict with the authorities. Any sensible person might ask, "Would it be possible to launch a movement of this kind and recruit thousands of supporters in a single day if the dead body of Jesus had really existed?" Peter preached his first sermon only a few hundred yards from His sepulcher. If Jesus' enemies had been in a position to prove that His body was still there, the sermon would have been a failure and would never have persuaded thousands of people to be baptized. But Jesus was not in the tomb. His enemies were powerless.

The apostles did not visit the tomb of Jesus because it had no significance as far as they were concerned. (Saul of Tarsus, after he was converted, came to Jerusalem and met the apostles but was not concerned with visiting the tomb, not even out of mere respect.) Nor did His enemies investigate the tomb to convince themselves and others that Jesus was still there. This is yet another proof that Jesus really rose from the dead. A great many people undertake pilgrimages to the tombs of minor saints. Even though the first apostles knew of this custom in Israel (Matthew 23:29), they were not interested in visiting Jesus' tomb because they knew it was empty.

All this was so universally accepted that the disciples started preaching, not in a provincial town where it would be difficult to check their statements, but in Jerusalem itself, arousing the enthusiasm of thousands of people and—what was still more remarkable—facing enemies who were impotent, because they were not in a position to deny that Jesus' tomb was empty. When the priests maintained that the body of Jesus had been stolen by the apostles, anyone could have answered them, "Why don't you arrest and sentence the men who have carried out this theft?"

The suggestion that Jesus did not actually die on the cross but merely fell into a deep swoon and recovered consciousness in the cool tomb is still more ridiculous. The soldiers saw that he was dead. Furthermore, how could He have pushed aside the stone, which had been sealed by the Roman authorities, and overpowered the guards after so much suffering? Could He have gone anywhere, naked as He was, with only a winding sheet for cover? He could have sought shelter only with one or more of His disciples. Had He done this, however, His disciples would have realized that He had not risen from the dead. Would they have been willing to give their lives for a lie they themselves had hatched?

We are compelled to believe what the Gospel writers say because they reveal such naivete when relating unflattering things about themselves. What induced them to spread abroad by word of mouth and in their writings that Peter, one of Jesus' closest friends, had been called "Satan" by his Master and had denied Him three times on the night that He was betrayed? The only motive I can discover is that they showed an uncompromising regard for the truth. The band of apostles was a collection of men who were guided by the truth. We can trust their evidence.

The remarkable thing is that when the apostles affirm the resurrection of Jesus to an audience of doubters (even in those days people were skeptical about stories of angels, resurrections, and so on), they merely affirm, without producing a single confirmatory piece of evidence. This was possible because what they maintained was a well-known and undisputed fact among the inhabitants of Jerusalem. After all, the risen Jesus had at one time appeared to five hundred persons, who must have had several thousand relatives with whom they shared their story.

The resurrection of Jesus can also be proved by two very famous conversions that could not be explained in any other way.

The first was the conversion of James, the brother of Jesus, to a faith in Him as the Messiah. While Jesus lived on earth, James did not believe in Him but considered Him to be out of His mind. The historian Josephus Flavius describes James as a very upright man. How was it possible that he became an apostle and martyr after the death of Jesus? Anyone reading James' letter will note that this is a Jewish letter, without any Christian characteristics. This leads us to realize that it was not the teaching of Jesus that made an impression on James and brought about his conversion.

What was the cause? It can only have been what we are told in the New Testament, that Jesus after His resurrection appeared to His brother and that the latter admitted his mistake and in remorse wrote the chapter in which he condemns his own former sin of judging and speaking against Jesus.

The second conversion was that of the rabbi Saul of Tarsus. This man had a vision on the road to Damascus in which Jesus appeared to him and spoke to him, whereupon Saul immediately became a disciple. Would this have been possible on purely psychological grounds? Even though Mohammed were to appear to me ten times, I would tell myself that I was suffering from hallucinations, and I certainly would not become a Mohammedan. Why should things have turned out so differently for the man who was to become the apostle Paul?

The truth is that he knew Jesus' tomb was empty, without being able to find a plausible explanation for this fact unless he admitted to himself that Jesus had risen. This was the crux of the matter: when he encountered Jesus, the last shred of doubt disappeared. He was converted. He later made his way to Jerusalem, but he had not the slightest intention of going to the tomb in order to shed tears of remorse there. He knew it was empty. He surely discussed with the apostles how to preach the resurrection. It would have been a psychological impossibility for the apostles, being the sort of men they were, to discuss how best to preach a lie.

Probably the most telling proof of the resurrection is the fact that millions of sinners in the history of mankind have changed their mind and become holy people. This miracle is happening daily in the Church. If you ask these people how this miracle of rebirth happened, their answer is always that Jesus did it. It is certain that it is a living Jesus, not a dead one, who has brought about these new births. I am one of these people.

The cumulative force of these arguments compels me to believe in the resurrection of Jesus. But let me turn to an argument from a person of real authority. Professor Theodor Mommsen, the great historian of the Roman Empire, wrote: "The resurrection of Jesus is the event in ancient history which has been more conclusively proved than any other event."

There is something more. If a woman's husband is missing in a war and believed to be dead, and then one, two, three, four people, in fact countless people, come and tell her that they have seen him in a prisoner-of-war camp, then the wife will trust those people. We are in the same situation. Those who believed that Christ was dead heard the witness of the women, of the apostles, of the disciples on the road to Emmaus, of five hundred people who had seen Him on the same day. After this it was only normal for them to believe that Jesus was no longer dead, but alive.

How Can You Contact Jesus Personally?

WHEN I FIRST heard sensible arguments for the existence of God and the resurrection of Jesus, I decided to find out for myself. I said, "I will pray—or rather un-pray—to the non-God."

I said in effect, "God, I know for sure that you do not exist. It would be nice to have somewhere a loving, almighty father. It is sad that You are only a figment of the imagination, a fancy of ignorant believers. But supposing that perchance You exist, it is not my duty to believe in You. It is Your duty to reveal Yourself to me. I have done many vain things in life. This prayer is one more link in the chain of stupid things I have said. I'm sorry about that, God. I would have preferred that You exist."

Well, this un-prayer was accepted. I read the Bible. I spoke with believers, not about their creeds but about their real experiences. Afterwards, I experienced some encounters myself. I am as sure that I have seen Jesus and heard Him speaking to me as I am sure of having spoken to my wife, though a tape recorder would have registered nothing. But have you never heard voices of persons who love or hate you much, encouraging and strengthening, or warning or threatening you? Aren't our perceptions broader than the sound-range of a machine?

Since every individual is different, encounters with Jesus also take different forms. I encourage you to try. If you wish, you can succeed.

I will tell you how one person came to have a personal fellowship with Jesus.

A pastor once asked a young man from a godly family who had drifted away from church, "Do you ever pray?"

He answered, "Never. I don't have anyone to pray to. No matter how loudly I shouted, those in the floor above me would not hear. I never had any sign that anyone in the air or beyond would be interested in listening to me."

The pastor told him, "I know you are interested in many sports, as well as art and science. You must also have many hobbies. I propose that you make an experiment. If it does not succeed, you have lost nothing except a few moments of your life—if one can say that an experiment with negative results is lost time. Dr. Wassermann made 605 negative experiments to find a remedy for syphilis. On the 606th he succeeded. Therefore the medicine against syphilis is called 606. The 605 negative experiments were not squandered efforts, but rather steps toward the discovery of truth.

"Tonight before going to bed, sit in a comfortable chair with an empty chair before you and imagine that Jesus sits in it. You know He is not there and consider Him long since dead, but you also know from general culture what He is believed to have been: a powerful, all-loving Son of God who came to earth to die for the sins of all mankind. It is a matter of record that He died on the cross. His adherents believe that He was resurrected and is alive. If—as I believe—He is God, He is omnipresent and can hear you.

"Never mind that you don't believe this. When Marco Polo returned from his travels in Asia in the fourteenth century and said he had been in places where men are yellow and have slanted eyes, that they write vertically instead of horizontally, he was called 'Marco Polo the liar.'

"There may be a grain of truth even in what everyone considers a lie.

"If the experiment has no result, you will have an amusing story to tell and will be more confirmed in your unbelief.

"Now, imagine that this Jesus, who is only a fancy, sits before you. What would you say if He were really there? Each of us leads imaginary conversations with members of our family who are not present or friends and loved ones far away. There is no one without such imaginary discussions.

"So imagine you are talking to Jesus. Don't use religious phrases. He is weary of religious cliches uttered by people without conviction. Those who sentenced Him to death had uttered beautiful prayers the night before. If you think His teachings are wrong, tell Him so. Tell Him that you consider Him a figment of your imagination and that you only amuse yourself, that you wish to lead a life of self-fulfillment in your trade and leisure. He has heard worse words. When His own people swore at Him, He was not angry at them. He knew their stage of spiritual development.

"I can assure you that what you say the first time will be just a monologue. But do it again the next day and say to Him, 'If you had a real existence, which I contest, I would have some earnest questions to put to you. What kind of God are You? You are said to be almighty and good. Then why all the tragedy and suffering in the world?'

"Tell Him the worst things you have endured in life. Carry on a monologue, with the other chair before you, about the evils in this world. By the way, you might remember to tell Him about some evils you yourself have done. There is no one else in the room. Just recount the evil done to you and by you. Such an emptying of the mind from the things that burden it is very useful, even if there is no one to listen." (In Freudian psychiatric sessions, the psychiatrist sits behind the patient so that he sees nobody.)

"On the third day, still with the armchair opposite you, speak to Him about the good and beautiful things you have encountered. You might remember that you have often neglected to show thankfulness. You have seen lovely flowers. You have met or read about great and good men. You wonder how such splendid characters and so many geniuses have developed in an evil world. Tell Him how amazed you are at the vastness of the sky and the multitude of stars. Mention the sun that gives light and life to evil and good alike.

"Think of how nice it would be if you could also be like them, spreading around you the light of joy, truth, and love. Ask Jesus how to be such a model of life.

"If you succeed in following all my suggestions and earnestly ask the question, 'How can I bring happiness into the lives of those I encounter and bring a smile to their lips?', your monologue will become a dialogue.

"I cannot tell you specifically what He will reply to you, because I am not Jesus. He knows that each person is unique and tailors His answer accordingly. But He will speak to you."

I know about one unbeliever who acted just as I have described above and came to converse with Jesus. He did so daily for many years. One present at his death recounted that his last gesture before dying was to stretch out his hand to his unseen Friend in that armchair which he always kept near his bed.

I have already given you proofs of Christ's resurrection. You can have one proof more, a decisive one: that you have talked with Him yourself.

Does God
Have a Son?

JESUS ACCREDITED Himself as God's messenger. He is acknowledged by Christians to be God's Son, which should not offend Muslims or Jews who believe in God but claim that He has no wife and does not procreate. If you are among these, understand that the appellation "Son" was never meant to be understood biologically.

The Jews of old had a language of few words. The Hebrew Bible has only 6,500 words, in contrast to the massive vocabulary of the English or German language. The word "Son" was used for many notions, for which we today have different words.

Son was used for "descendant." Jesus was called the Son of David though He was twenty-eight generations removed from him. It was also used for "disciple," as in the Biblical expression "sons of the prophets."

The Hebrew language was especially limited in adjectives. The Jews called hot-tempered people "sons of thunder" (Mark 3:17), and peaceful men "sons of peace" (Luke 10:6). Generally male believers are called "sons of God" (2 Corinthians 6:18).

Don't be offended at expressions used thousands of years ago by men of an entirely different culture. Simply understand that believing souls who met Jesus experienced an encounter with God. They said to themselves that if God were to walk on earth as a man, He would be like Jesus. They knew they had met God.

Can God's Existence Be Proved?

ISN'T THE notion "God" false?

Well, I never had any proof that I exist, that I have a brain or lungs. But surely I do exist. If not, who is the one who asks the question? I breathe, therefore I have lungs. I think, therefore I have a brain.

I perceive a reality apart, which in religion is called "God."

Do I perceive Him as I perceive other realities? Would video cameras record this presence? No. Then doesn't this make me doubt what I experience? No, because it is a perception much more intense than everyday realities I experience. The power with which this presence impacts me goes beyond all the limits of human technique. It also exceeds the very limited power of the human mind. The apostle Paul, a deep thinker in matters of religion, calls man's wisdom "the foolishness of God" because God goes beyond human reason. He also belongs to another sphere.

Columbus discovered a world unknown to Europeans. God's children have also discovered a reality unknown to others.

We cannot put much of this experience in human words, because the vocabulary of all languages comes from sense perceptions. But there is also a supersensory reality. We had a glimpse of the Creator and then received through Jesus His revelation for mankind.

No arguments for the existence of God are needed. What argument do we need for the existence of existence?

Make Great Plans

YOU ARE right to desire changes in society. The best revolutionaries are those who start on themselves. Therefore become a light yourself.

You wish the good of your race, religion, class, party, country, but you use your energy within the limits of only a small portion of reality. Other races, classes, nations, religions, and parties have their own agenda, and you will find yourself in conflict with them. The end result will be as much unhappiness as before. Therefore don't make small plans.

Jesus lived as a Man among men. He was a poor, unknown carpenter. What if He had applied His power to save the Jews from Roman oppression? The Jews were a small people. If they had defeated the Romans, the Greeks or another empire would have oppressed them. What if Jesus had fought the existing religious institutions in which truth had been corrupted? More recent history provides an example. Centuries ago there was a struggle to overthrow Catholicism, which had suffered corruption. As a result, Protestantism arose, which has gone the same route of corruption.

A small group of Serbian terrorists wanted a free Serbian state of their own, without belonging to the Austro-Hungarian monarchy. Therefore they killed the Austrian crown prince. The result was World War I, in which all continents were involved and ten million died. The whole political structure of the world was altered. Seventy years have passed since the incident. Today Serbia is much worse off than it once was. In retrospect, was it wise for the terrorists to murder the Archduke Ferdinand?

Jesus says that His intention is "to save the world" (John 3:17), not to destroy it. If His purpose is achieved by us, there would be true peace and happiness. It would be wise to make Jesus' universal plan of salvation your own.

There exists in the universe the law of unintended consequences: in a complex system it is not always possible to predict what the consequences of any change will be.

Terrorists use stone-age methods in twentieth-century society. Savages knew only how to throw a stone or hurl a spear at the enemy. They had no language skills for negotiating with an adversary. In fact, even today there are primitive tribes with a vocabulary of only a few hundred words. Without such words as sympathy, tenderness, compromise, how could they come to an understanding with their fellow men?

Today most nations have a rich vocabulary and various means of communication: the printed word, radio, TV, even a knowledge of psychology. Talk is a much more efficient means of solving problems than violence.

The heart of many men is like a dark cellar full of cockroaches, termites, and snakes. We men are limited and therefore can never find a solution valid for all the problems of the world. Jesus is an exceptional being. He demonstrated a truth adequate under all circumstances and in all ages. It is love and faith.

With his limitations man can only provide remedies of limited value. But Jesus has the key to the kingdom of eternal peace and holiness because He is both human and divine. He has been rightly identified as the Son of God.

The majority of those who knew Him when He walked on earth refused His message. They preferred their sins and their petty enmities to divine love. Sin crucified Jesus two thousand years ago. Sin still kills today.

You will agree with the Bible when it speaks about the evil in men. You rightly consider your adversaries to be evil. But the Bible also asserts that "the best of men are like a briar" (Micah 7:4). You too need repentance and forgiveness.

In our knowledge of the universe and of man himself, we have only scratched the surface. About our own selves we have scant knowledge. One virus or one sudden burst of unreasonableness—and who does not have such?—can destroy all our plans. To serve mankind successfully, we need God's wisdom.

Who Is Your
Adversary...Your Friend?

WHILE IN prison in Nuremberg, Goering (Hitler's right-hand man) was asked before being sentenced to death, "How is it that the mightiest German army, with the best generals and finest armaments, has suffered an unprecedented total defeat, surrendering unconditionally?"

He replied, "We did not know how powerful the Soviet army was or that the Western armies would ally themselves with it." Lack of knowledge ruined Hitler's plan to erect his thousand-year empire.

How much do you really know? Won't you end up on the gallows like the Nazi leaders or in jail because you did not know well your adversaries, or even the head of your own trusted organization? And what if he proves to be unreliable?

In the Bible we read that the eyes of God run to and fro over all the earth. He is the only One who has foresight, insight, hindsight, throughsight, the only One who sees all aspects of a thing or situation. If you take God as your guide, you cannot fail.

Since man was created for a Christlike life, it is our duty to live this life. Because we have not lived up to this ideal it does not mean that we have lost all chance for change. When Jesus died on the cross, He prayed that His crucifiers might be forgiven. In tistory of mankind there has never been a sin greater than this: to kill the One who has come to save. But if even this sin can be forgiven, then all of our sins can be forgiven. When one of the thieves crucified near Him entreated for forgiveness, Jesus readily forgave him and promised him a place in paradise.

One can object that if the worst of criminals can be so easily forgiven, justice is no longer possible. If a person is obliged to give to whoever asks—without discerning if he is entitled to ask—then one has no defense against a robber. If everyone turned the other cheek when physically abused, if thieves who stole one thing were recompensed with something even more precious, society would soon disintegrate. In fact, criminals would flourish in a society where evil deeds are rewarded.

We understand that you would have a hard time adapting to such all-forgiving and all-embracing love. But Jesus knew that mankind, as it is, could not live according to these laws.

These are precepts for a special category of people who are spiritually beyond the average person. They have passed through a new experience: they have received a new heart. The very seat of sentiments, emotions, and high thoughts has been changed. Such individuals are spiritually born again, though physically they continue to be citizens of this world.

But just as geniuses are beyond the intellectual level of their fellows, so Jesus' disciples are qualitatively beyond other men, because in them the character of their Master is embodied. They have identified with Him as His body. He works through them. They have a calling different from the rest of the world.

The marrow of Jesus' teachings is the idea of substitution. In crucifixion, He substituted Himself for sinners. He identified with them. He bore the punishment for our sins and thus obtained forgiveness and cleanliness for us. He has risen from the dead and ascended to heaven, but the world is not without His visible presence. We are now called to do His exceptional works—yea, even greater ones than His—to speak His words, to bring His peace to a troubled world.

He is our substitute before the heavenly Father. We identify with the Holiest of all, and He identifies with us because we are one with Him. All of His righteousness is attributed to us. We bring into the world His love. In exchange, He has taken upon Himself all of our sins as if He had committed them. He became the personification of human sin, enduring on the cross the punishment we deserved. Our ugly past is washed away. Through Him we become white as snow.

We can have fellowship with God as with a loving father; we have angels as our ministers. We are called upon to be lights in the world. The rules in the Sermon on the Mount are for us.

Only we can accomplish them. We will work on ourselves more and more as Christ leads us in order to obtain His character. This can be the content of our whole earthly life.

Other men's striving for self-improvement is vain. For what purpose is all of their effort? To prepare for the grave? But we know that this life is only an episode preparatory to an eternal one. It is a prologue. We prepare ourselves for blessings without end.

The Real Revolution

MICHELANGELO was opposed to painting a portrait of a maid if she lacked classic beauty. In his works of art he eliminated the imperfections of nature. So we must allow Jesus to eliminate from us everything that is imperfect.

This is the revolution to be accomplished.

Terrorists are opposed to rulers, governments, rich men, captains of industry, and so on. Christians desire to be men "after God's own heart"—men of love. We recommend this to you as well.

Terrorists are not isolated individuals or groups. They express very widespread feelings. In Italy, a certain Pietro Maso killed his parents. While in jail, he received hundreds of letters of solidarity for his revolutionist courage, despite the fact that he belonged to a dangerous species. Civilization has at once reached the highest peak of artistic sensibility and the lowest depth of mindless bestiality.

We call you, our friends, to the highest: to be Christlike. We pray you may accept this calling. But there is an old maxim of wisdom: "What cannot be turned to good must at least be kept from being very bad."

Francis of Assisi was told that bandits had settled in the forest near his monastery and that they were a threat to the lives of worshipers. He was asked, "Should we call the police?"

He answered, "No. Instead, go to them with some food and wine and tell them, 'Francis blesses you and asks one thing of you. He understands that you cannot change your lives all at once. He understands that you cannot do without stealing. But promise at least not to kill.'" This they promised. After a time, he asked them not to steal at least on Sundays and on great feasts because then many worshipers came to church. Thus successively he convinced them to give up stealing.

I knew a wise Christian mother whose son had become a robber. She was unable to bring him to conversion, but he listened to her when she advised him to change from robber to pickpocket. "Robbers can be shot when they break into houses and can also be tempted to shoot. A pickpocket's life is safer," she told him. He was convinced. Later he also gave up being a pickpocket.

It is always good to make worthwhile steps to improve yourself a step at a time. But there exists also the possibility of a total inner revolution.

You can have complete forgiveness in a moment for every wrong you have ever done. You can also obtain a new character that will make you a blessing to others and will fit you for a beautiful life here and in eternity.

Jesus, Your Friend

I END WITH the thought with which I began. Many look at terrorists with fear, others with hate. Jesus fears and hates no one. Like God who gives sunshine and rain to all, so He loves and desires to forgive and save all. You can rely on Him as on a friend.

The story is told of two brothers who once lived completely opposite lives. The older was a God-fearing man, good to everyone. The younger was rebellious, even violent. The older brother tried to influence him, but in vain.

One evening, while the older sat quietly in his home, the brother stormed in with blood on his clothes, shouting, "Save me if you can! I have killed a man and the police are after me!"

The older replied, "Quick! Let's change clothes."

They did so. The murderer donned the white garment, and the innocent put on the blood-stained one.

Scarcely had they finished when the police arrived. Seeing the older brother in bloody clothes, they knew they had found their man and dragged him from his home. They had no doubt that he was the one they sought.

Brought to court, the accused admitted his guilt. The judge bowed to what seemed clear evidence and sentenced him to death.

He had one last wish: "At the moment of my execution, please give my brother this letter." His wish was granted.

Later, when the brother opened the letter, he read: "I died in your place, in your bloody garment, for your guilt. I was happy to make this sacrifice for you and ask only one thing, that you live a life of love and goodness."

The innocent was dead. Nothing could change that fact. But as often as former comrades asked the younger to participate in an act of violence, he replied, "I cannot do it in the white garment I received from the brother who died for me."

This is exactly what Jesus did for each one of us. He Himself was without any sin. But He took upon Himself the sins of us all and bore our punishment as He expired on the cross. His blood can cleanse you from all of your sins, just as He cleansed me from mine. Believe in Him and you will be saved from hate and despair. He will make you a child of God who will spread love and light.

So says God in His holy book, the Bible.

A Law of the Other World

BESIDES THE visible, palpable world, there also exists a world of ideals, aspirations, hopes, sentiments, reason, and intuition. There is the world of the spirit, which is different from the material world.

The metaphysical realm has laws very different from those of the world we perceive with our senses.

In this world everyone has to deal with the consequences of their own decisions. Not so in God's world where love reigns. Love always identifies with the beloved. Jesus, the perfect Son of God, became sin out of love for sinners. For their part, sinners who love Him to the point of receiving Him become sons and daughters of God in His image. It is an exchange of garments.

In the spiritual world, a Lover can take upon Himself the guilt of others just as if it were His own. In return, the guilty obtains the lily-whiteness of the Lover, who is Jesus.

You might be burdened with the remembrance of some very evil deed you have committed, and you might ask yourself if God's pardon extends to someone like you.

Be confident! No human sin can be greater than God's grace.

Once a very poor girl from a small town went to the big city to earn some money to support her old mother. Soon after her arrival, she realized that an attractive girl can earn more money without working than by honest work.

Recognizing her own assets, she became all too successful. She pleased men and soon had money, jewels, and a life of revelry. Her mother was forgotten. What does a mother count when one dances to popular tunes?

Years passed by. One day she was stricken with remorse and asked herself, "I wonder how my mother is. I have neglected her completely."

She took the first train to her old village, arriving late at night. To her amazement, she found the gate of her house wide open. She mother was always careful to lock it at night. Then she saw a light burning in the window of her mother's bedroom. A lamp burning so late? Mother usually went to bed early. Might she be sick?

When she crossed the threshold, she heard her mother's voice: "Joan, is that you?"

"Yes, mother," she replied. "But how is it that the gate is wide open so late at night?"

"Since you left, the gate has not been closed."

"But why is the light burning so late? Why aren't you asleep?"

"Since you left, it has never been extinguished. A loving mother's heart waited for you."

You can be sure that when you desire to knock at the gate of heaven, it will be wide open to receive you. The light of a Father's love will shine upon you. The return of a prodigal son or daughter will be feasted with great joy by God and the heavenly beings. He awaits you with great longing.

To be a serene, loving child of God, desirous of pleasing Him and sharing His goodness with others, is far better than committing acts of terror.

God allowed His Son to die in your place. Jesus is your best Friend. Come to Him!

Your idea of changing things in the world to more justice is good. I work at this, too. Start by changing yourself.

For questions or information, you may write to:

P.O. Box 443
Bartlesville, OK 74005